TO PLAY AND PRAY

Twenty ideas for Teachers

by John Harris-Douglas
and Michael Kindred

CIO PUBLISHING
Church House, Dean's Yard, Westminster, SW1P 3NZ

ISBN 0 7151 0386 5

Printed in England by Bocardo & Church Army Press Ltd, Cowley, Oxford,
England.

CONTENTS

Page

Introduction

The importance in our lives of playing games is now well documented. For many of us involved in teaching or sharing the Christian Faith, our task is so important to us that we often forget that it should be fun—if we can possibly make it so. For the young in particular, learning should be an enriching experience.

Our Lord told many stories to try to help people to understand the truths he wished to share with them. In *To Play and Pray,* we have collected ideas which we hope will help children to have fun in their learning and perhaps to discover new aspects of the Christian Faith. These ideas are designed to be fun vehicles, or aids to teaching: they have their limitations but, used imaginatively, they can be of help in school, group or church.

In order to keep down costs we have not produced apparatus: this is also a self-help book!

Michael Kindred and I have tried these ideas with children and teachers—and found they work! After some twenty years spent in RE teaching, I find this type of aid invaluable. Like pictures, models, films, records, these games and simulations help us to share our knowledge and understandings in ways that enable our children to discover a little more about Jesus, and to share more happily in the Christian fellowship in which they are growing up.

Sometimes it is enough just to look at a picture, listen to some music, to be with someone or to play a game. But there are times when we need to stop for a moment, to think, to try to put thoughts or feelings into words.

In using these games we have felt the need to 'offer them in prayer', to remind ourselves we have played for a good purpose in God's good time.

I have tried to place these games in the context of prayer. Please read the 'pointer' prayer or suggestion yourself BEFORE you begin! Afterwards, you will know better whether or not to use them All-together.

We shall be glad of any findings, experiences, suggestions from those of you who use these ideas: please send them to us.

John Harris-Douglas
Brafferton, York

Most of the ideas, games and simulations in this book were devised originally for the 'Sunday School' (perish the phrase!), and Youth Forum at St Martin's Church in Bilborough, Nottingham. A few, with certain modifications, were used with our adult Discovery Group (A name we coined which we felt expressed the purpose of the group).

Over the few years involved, none of us realised that the children, young people and adults in these various groups were acting as guinea pigs in testing them out. I am very grateful to all of them for all their help and patience—and tolerance. Naturally, some ideas we tried out were ineffective and fell by the wayside. (Some were disastrous and fell very heavily!)

The ideas originated mainly because we had the kind of children and older people who preferred to learn by more informal, practical methods, where experience is the teacher, and where you can have fun. Having fun is a most important aspect of learning. Another is that the experience should be as memorable as possible. We hope you will find both of these elements present. Some of the ideas may be new. Some are different combinations of ideas that have been around for some time.

The story of how I eventually became involved in working together with John Harris-Douglas in producing this book is too complicated to explain here. It is sufficient to say that I'm glad this co-operation has happened, as he has been able to inject much valuable content into the games and simulations I have devised. Various people have helped me on the way, and I would like to thank the Wadderton Group for their initial encouragement.

In looking through the ideas that follow, and perhaps in using them, you may find that various trains of thought are set off in your mind, which could lead to the development of your own ideas. This is the kind of 'spin-off' we hope you will experience. To this end, we have not indicated what age ranges we think various ideas are suitable for, as this could tend to limit your own creative ability in adapting an idea for your own local situation. Where we have used 'children', for example, feel free to substitute 'Young people' or 'adults' and see how the game would then work.

There has been no attempt to arrange the ideas into any kind of course, thematic or otherwise. This isn't that kind of book. It's meant to be a resource book to help you to inject new ideas into your groups when you feel it is appropriate.

Those who are wanting to use an idea once only, with one specific group, may find the preparation a little daunting in some cases. Please don't be put off! It's true to say that in some kinds of teaching, and learning, the preparation takes longer than the lesson.

Anyway, we hope you may find something of value in this book. May we wish you every success in using or adapting any of the material contained in the following pages.

Michael Kindred

Jesus uses Us

1. Ask the children to draw a square on a piece of paper, so that the side of the square is about 2½". While they are doing this, draw the square yourself to a much larger scale on a sheet of newsprint or similar paper which you have previously put on the wall.

2. Now ask them to divide the square into 5 squares by 5 squares— show them on the one you have drawn.

3. Now ask them to carefully put the letters in as shown below:

```
S   U   S   U   S
U   S   E   S   U
S   E   J   E   S
U   S   E   S   U
S   U   S   U   S
```

4. Ask them how many times they can spell out the word 'US' starting from each letter 'U' in the square. The word may be spelt backwards as well as forwards, upwards as well as downwards. Allow them about 3 or 4 minutes. Tell them to write their answer down.

5. The next word they have to find is 'USES'. How many times can they spell out this word, starting from each letter 'U' in turn? Again, words may be spelt in any direction as before. 3 or 4 minutes allowed again— answer to be written down.

6. Finally, starting with the letter 'J' in the middle, how many times can they spell out the word 'JESUS'? Words to be spelt in any direction as before. Answers to be written down after three or four minutes.

7. Underneath your own square on the board, at the right hand end of the sheet of paper, write the word US. Go round the children in turn and ask them how many times they found the word. Then write the answer under the word US, which is 24.

8. In the centre of your large paper under the square, write the word USES. Ask the children for their answers as before. Write down the correct answer underneath the word USES which is 48.

9. Finally put the word JESUS at the left hand side, ask for the answers and then write the correct answer under JESUS, which is 48. The answers on your paper should look like this:

JESUS   USES   US
  48   48   24

10. Ask any of the children who are good at arithmetic to multiply all three numbers together! The answer is 55,296.

11.   Help them to see that they found JESUS USES US in lots of different ways in the square of letters. From this, lead on to the idea that they may find JESUS USES US in lots of different ways in our lives—if we let him!

NB   Some children may like to know the easier ways of counting up the number of times each word occurs. Tell them that the square of letters is the same whichever way you look at it—it is symmetrical. Therefore you can count how many times the word US comes from one of the Us (which is 3) and then multiply by the number of U's in the square.

When Jesus lived on earth, the gospel stories tell us that he used his eyes clearly to look at people and the world about them.
He used his hands to work, to help and care.
Jesus used his feet to take him to the places where he was needed, where it was good for him to be.
Jesus loved God and his fellow men with all his heart.
And now,
Jesus needs our eyes, our hands, our feet, our hearts, to keep on with his work each day.
Let us pray:

> Use our eyes, Lord Jesus, to smile and know the truth:
> Use our hands, Lord Jesus, to work and help and heal.
> Use our feet, Lord Jesus, along your promised way,
> Use our hearts, Lord Jesus, to love more day by day:

Amen.

9

Jesus on the Cross

General Outline
This is a fairly simple visual aid to help children to remember a little about the events in Jerusalem on Maundy Thursday and Good Friday.

Requirements
One piece of thickish white or coloured card per child, prepared before the lesson by the teacher as shown in the diagram: (Actual size)

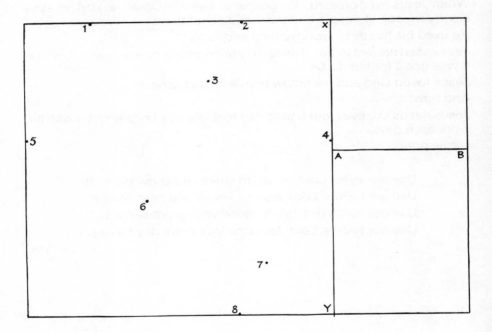

Each child will also need the use of a pencil, a straight-edge or ruler, and a pair of scissors.

Procedure
1. Tell the children that this little puzzle will help them to remember something about what happened to Jesus from the time when he prayed in the Garden of Gethsemane on Maundy Thursday to his crucifixion on Good Friday.

10

2. Now ask them to join up the following points on the sheet of card by a pencil line:
- (a) point 1 to point 4, passing through point 3.
- (b) point 5 to point 7, passing through point 6.
- (c) point 2 to point 6, passing through point 3.
- (d) point 7 to point 8.
- (e) point 1 to point 5.

3. Now ask them to cut the card up as follows:—
- (a) Cut along the line X–Y.
- (b) Cut along the line A–B and keep the uppermost square—the other piece can be discarded.
- (c) On the small square you have just cut off put the letters U and S as shown in Diagram 2. Then put the letters G and G as shown.
- (d) Now put the letter E, sloping as shown in the top right hand piece in the large square, with a small letter M just below it.
- (e) Now put the letter S shown in the upper left with the smaller letters A and L further over to the right.
- (f) A small D wants to go near the right hand edge at the bottom.
- (g) Now put a large J in the bottom left corner, with the letters E, R and U over to its right.

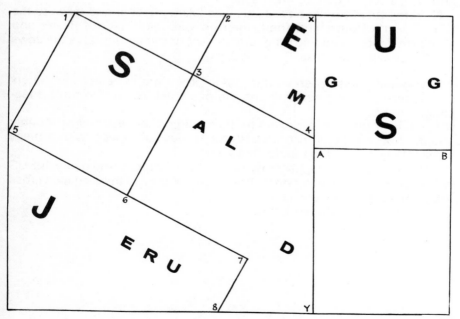

11

4.   The next cuts are to be made along the pencil lines which were drawn in No. 2 above. This cuts the large square up into six pieces.

5.   Now make sure that the children each have the large square with all its pieces fitted together as they were before they cut them out, and to have the small square a little away at the side.

6.   Tell them that the large square represents the City of Jerusalem on the night of Maundy Thursday. The letters are in disorder to show that the city itself was partly in disorder because the Jewish authorities were plotting to capture Jesus and kill him. Hidden in the city is JUDAS. Ask the children to find the letters which make up Judas, hidden in the letters on the large square.
     Now look at the small square. The two letters 'G' represent the Garden of Gethsemane. Jesus was there on Maundy Thursday evening, praying very hard about all the terrible things he knew he was to face very soon. He was there in the Garden, praying, because he cared about US (the other two letters in the small square).
     Then Judas came out of Jerusalem with a band of men to the Garden of Gethsemane to betray Jesus.
     Now ask the children to move the pieces in the large square around out of place—don't turn them over!—and move them across in a haphazard way towards the Garden of Gethsemane—representing the band of men and Judas coming out to find Jesus.
     Now tell them briefly how Jesus was taken prisoner and taken to the High Priest's House and tried, then he was taken before Pilate, and although Pilate could find no wrong in him, he eventually gave the Jews what they wanted—Jesus for crucifying.

7.   Now ask them to solve the puzzle! They are to rearrange the six pieces from the large square and the one small square, to form a tee-shaped cross.
N.B.   It is important to explain to the children that Jesus was probably crucified on a cross which consisted of an upright piece, with a piece horizontally across the top, forming a letter T.
     If they have difficulty, give them a clue! The letters of the name JESUS will appear in their correct order from top to bottom of the T-shaped cross if they have solved it correctly.
     The solution is shown below.

8. Now explain that from Jerusalem, Jesus carried his cross, possibly with some help, out to the hill of Calvary, and here we see in the solution of the puzzle, JESUS on the Cross.

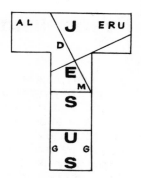

Ask them to notice that the solution needs the small square with US at the bottom to be correct, and this represents US coming to the foot of the cross. At the foot of the Cross we see ourselves as part of his sacrifice.

We have just done a type of jig-saw of the saddest part of Jesus' life: the part we remember especially on Maundy Thursday and Good Friday.

As piece by piece we learn the story of Jesus, we see how the pieces fit together; we see how and why Jesus was hurt and killed. We know that this is not the end of the story, because there is Easter Day to come. Perhaps we should remember that there are other parts to come for our lives too, especially when everything seems bad or sad.

But let us thank God for Jesus' life as we pray:

Dear God,

       We thank you for the life of your Son Jesus, for his courage, his strength to be hurt for us all. We thank you for his laughter, his teaching and his work.

       Especially now we thank you for his dying and his living.

Amen.

Evangelising the World in a Month!

Obviously, this is not to be taken too seriously!—but by using extremes, the children may grasp the idea of how the Gospel—the Good News—of Jesus Christ, may be spread by those who have already grasped a little of what it is about, to those who know nothing at all about it. It is also interesting to discuss how 'bad news' can spread very rapidly, especially in these days of television and the other mass communication systems.

You may like to introduce this little exercise by telling the children about the legend of the King who wished to reward one of his most faithful servants and called him to the Royal Chamber. He asked the servant what reward he would like. The servant, after a moment's thought, asked the King for a chess board to be set down in front of them. The King was puzzled and intrigued, but complied with the servant's request. The servant then asked for his reward: 'I should be grateful to his Majesty if he would give me one grain of corn for the first square on the board, two grains for the second square, four grains for the third square, and so on, doubling the amount of corn each time until the sixty-fourth square is reached.' The King, who was no mathematician, laughed long and loud. 'Of course you may have such a reward,' said the King, 'Bring in a sack of corn.' He felt he was getting away lightly by giving what seemed such a small reward. Imagine his surprise and dismay when he realised that there was not enough corn in the world with which to reward his servant!

Tell the children that all they will need, besides pencil and paper, is the ability to multiply by 2. (The paper should preferably be ruled, narrow feint, A4 size.)

Ask them to write the word January on the first line at the left, at the top of the page. Then at the side of January write '1st'. Then on the second line write '2nd' and so on, as on the diagram on the next page, finishing with February 1st.

Over the column next to the dates, tell them to put the heading:—'Total number of people to whom some knowledge of the Gospel has been spread.'

Now tell them that on January 1st they are to imagine that only one person has knowledge of the Gospel. On that day, that one person tells one other person what he knows of the Gospel. Tell them to put a figure 2 towards the right hand side of the column opposite January 1st.

Now ask them to put in the right hand column a description which helps to give them some idea of the number of people involved. This becomes more helpful as the total number gets bigger. For 2, they could put 'Mother and Father', or 'My sister and I'—(They would be more likely to write: 'Me and my sister'!).

They should now move on to January 2nd. Explain that the two people who had some knowledge of the Gospel from the previous day, now each tell one other person something about it. How many are now 'in the know'? When they have all agreed on the answer '4', tell them to write it under the '2'. Again, they should think of some description which helps to give them an idea of the size of the group now involved. They may put something like 'Average size of a family in Britain'.

This process continues with each of the days, as shown below. Examples of descriptions which give some idea of the number of people involved each day, have been suggested.

Emphasise that the final figure of 4,294,967,296 is about the size of the population of the world for the year 1976.

Total number of people to whom some knowledge of the Gospel has been spread.			*Sample Description*
January	1st	2	Mother and Father
	2nd	4	Average size of a family in Britain
	3rd	8	A boat team in the Oxford-Cambridge Boat Race
	4th	16	First-team pool of a football club
	5th	32	About the size of a class of children
	6th	64	
	7th	128	
	8th	256	Approx. no. C. of E. clergy in average diocese
	9th	512	About 100 less than number of MPs.
	10th	1,024	
	11th	2,048	
	12th	4,096	Average gate, 3rd Division football match
	13th	8,192	
	14th	16,384	Average gate, 2nd Division football match
	15th	32,768	Average gate, 1st Division football match
	16th	65,536	
	17th	131,072	About ⅓ more than a Wembley crowd

15

18th	... ...	262,144	Nearly the population of Nottingham
19th	... ...	524,288	A few more than the number of Jews in Britain
20th	...	1,048,576	
21st	...	2,097,152	
22nd	...	4,194,304	
23rd	...	8,388,608	Nearly the population of Greater London
24th	...	16,777,216	
25th	...	33,554,432	
26th	...	67,108,864	About 10 million more than U.K. population
27th	...	134,217,728	Nearly the population of Japan
28th	...	268,435,456	About the population of the United States
29th	...	536,870,912	Nearly the population of India
30th	...	1,073,741,824	
31st	...	2,147,483,648	
February 1st	...	4,294,967,296	*About World Population size in 1976*

In the 'Sample Descriptions' you will need to let children make suggestions so that you can eliminate the unhelpful ones, before they write anything down in that column.

Discussion points

1. Which spreads faster, bad news or good news? Give reasons.

2. How did Jesus spread his Good News? How did his twelve disciples play a part in this? How did other people play their part?

3. Who are the people in your life who have helped to give you a glimpse of the Good News of Jesus Christ?

NB The sample descriptions above are based, in the main, on figures available in almanacks, etc., and were prepared in February 1977.

It would be interesting to make some almanacks available to the children so that they could discover relevant figures for themselves on which they could base their own sample descriptions.

Bad news spreads faster than good news.

A disaster hits the headlines. Happiness and success seldom do.

Is this why we are so slow at telling and sharing the Good News of Jesus? But he tells us to speak his Gospel to all the world: so we must get on with it, however many people there are.

Dear God,
Help us to spread the good news of your love for us,
to tell the story of Jesus and to share with other people,
the strength,
the happiness,
the hope,
which comes from belonging
to Jesus, now and every day. Amen.

Compass Points Game

1.   Arrange the children in a circle sitting on chairs with a small table in the middle of the circle. Fix a piece of paper at least 18" square to the top of the table using Sellotape or similar adhesive tape. Mark a point in the centre of the paper using a felt-tipped marker pen.

2.   Now ask the children in turn to draw a line from the central point in the direction which they think is magnetic north. They are to put a small arrow on the end of the line and write their name or initials at the end of the arrow. Notice whether children blindly follow any of the arrows which have been drawn before their turn, or whether they try to think it out for themselves.
   Sometimes, if you get a fair number of lines close together, children will tend to go with the majority when it is their turn.

3.   When all have finished, place a compass over the central point and see which child was the nearest. Remember not to have any metal objects near to the compass! How many were near misses? How many were nowhere near?

4.   Now Sellotape another piece of paper on the table. (First removing the piece you have already used).

5.   Now ask them to draw, in turn, an arrow which points to either south-east or south-west. Can they use the information they have already gained to supply the new information? (Choose a different child to start this time)

6.   Again, when all have finished, place the compass on the central point and check the guesses for accuracy.

7.   Remove this piece of paper, and Sellotape another one in its place.

8.   Now ask them to draw a line in the direction of a large city which is more than about 50 miles away. If your Sunday School is in London, you may ask them to draw arrows in the direction of Birmingham.

9.   This time you will need to place a map of Britain carefully over the sheet of paper so that your city or town is over the central point, thereby giving you the direction of the city to which the arrows are supposed to be pointing. (You will of course need to use your compass to orientate the map.)

10.   This process may be repeated if you like, on another piece of paper, with any well-known city abroad, but of course for this you will need a small-scale map of the world to check the guesses.

Discussion Points

1. How did they make their choice of direction of line each time? Did they look at what had been drawn previously and 'follow the crowd'. Did they, for the attempts following the first round, use the information they had obtained when they were shown which was north?

2. How do we know what direction to take in the various things we do in life? How do we choose between the 'right' way and the 'wrong' way? Is there necessarily a right and wrong way sometimes? Do we need gradually to acquire knowledge—and the wisdom to use that knowledge—to help us decide which direction to go in the many choices we face in life?

3. Jesus said 'Follow me'. He didn't just mean that the person concerned was to walk behind him, blindly following him. What did he mean?

4. If you are the kind of person who advises other people about the choices they should make, or helps them to find out in what direction to go at particular stages in their lives, thus influencing others, how important it is to be right? What do you mean by 'right'? How do you decide whether you are right? How important is it to give thought to how you are leading others?

Do you know what a helter-skelter is? You climb to the top of a tower, sit on a mat, and come down the slippery slide which goes round and round the outside of the tower.

Sometimes life can feel like such a ride, going round and round, down and down: but it isn't just exciting or fun because we know our slide is getting us further into a mess; perhaps more and more problems, more and more lies.

God knows that life is sometimes like that, and so he promised to help us all if we will let him.

In the Old Testament part of the Bible there is the story of Joshua who had to lead his people into a strange land; he was frightened. Read God's promise in the Book of Joshua, chapter 1, verse 9.

In the New Testament Jesus told his disciples to go out into all the world and tell people about God and his new way of life—The Good News Way.

Read Jesus' promise in St. Matthew's Gospel, chapter 28, verse 20.

Dear God,

Thank you for your promises to be with us through Jesus at all times. Help us to remember this especially when we are frightened or alone, when we feel lost or tempted to do wrong things.

Help us to follow the 'Good News Way' of Jesus Christ, today and every day.

Amen.

The Handicap Simulation

Each child is going to pretend to be handicapped in some way, e.g. blind, leg in splint, thumb hurt, etc. You will need sufficient scarves and bandages, (the latter perhaps cut from old sheets, etc.), to simulate this.

You will also need some household objects which require hand, arm or leg movements to operate them or use them, e.g.:—knife, fork, spoon and plate; saucepans; a coat; 'pretend' coin and paper money; a reading lamp and a bulb; an old transistor radio; a tie; three or four nuts and bolts.

Divide the children into small groups, preferably with four or five in each group. You will need one small table per group, onto which the various household objects can be put. Two or three objects per table should be sufficient.

Tell the children that they are going to experience something of what it is like to be handicapped. Distribute sufficient bandages per group so that they can 'handicap' members as follows:—

(a)   One member has both thumbs bandaged up. The thumbs should be bent in towards the palms so that there is no possibility of their being brought into use. The bandages should be wrapped round the hand so that just the fingers are exposed.

(b)   Another member has all his fingers bandaged up-on both hands. A simple bandage round all four fingers on each hand will suffice.

(c)   Another member has a sling put round the arm and hand he uses most in the careful manipulation of objects. (Let any ambidextrous members suffer the other handicaps—not this one!)

(d)   The fourth member of the group is blindfolded.

(e)   If there is a fifth member, he should have one leg in a splint—a short length of wood will help to simulate this.

Each group starts at one of the tables, and each member, in turn, tries to use or operate the objects on the table. After two or three minutes, each group moves on to the next table. This process is repeated until each group has visited each table.

Discussion

It is helpful if the bandages, etc., are left on for the discussion, except in the case of those who have been blindfolded, as it helps the feelings experienced during the simulation to be retained more easily.

1.   How did each person feel about their particular handicap? What difficulties were experienced in using and operating the various objects? How did these difficulties vary with each handicap and each object?

2.   Why did Jesus show concern for handicapped people?—Can you find out from the Bible? Which Handicapped people were we told he met?

3.   Are there any people today who show a special concern for those with handicaps? (They may range from Mother Teresa to the child who reads to Granny because she can't see).

We may not think that we have a handicap: we may have good eye-sight, hearing, legs and arms. Our minds, too, may be clear and strong. But we all have some handicaps. We may not be able to speak well on the telephone, or tie bows; we may be frightened of heights or get tired quickly at football; we may be shy with other people, or not able to understand their point of view.

So let us always remember each other, whatever our handicap may be. (If we still think we haven't got one, perhaps we should think again!)

Dear Father God,
    Thank you for good minds and strong bodies, but even more for warm and loving hearts. Help us to help each other, whether our handicaps be big or small. Help us to be each other's eyes, each other's ears and hands, to share our talents or our strengths.
    Alone we are weak, together we are stronger, and with you we are truly strong.
    Thank you, God. Amen.

'I am with you always'.

1.   Prepare 25 square cards, say 1½" × 1½". With a felt marker pen put a large letter 'J' on five of them, a letter 'E' on another five, the letter 'U' on five, and the letter 'S' on the remaining ten. (Make sure that the letters don't show through the other side of the cards).

2.   Without the children seeing you do it, place the cards *face down* on a table in the order shown below:

```
J   E   S   U   S
J   E   S   U   S
J   E   S   U   S
J   E   S   U   S
J   E   S   U   S
```

3.   Ask a child to pick any card by pointing to the back of it. Remove the card and place it on one side. Then remove all the other cards which were in the same row and column as the card chosen, and discard them.

4.   Now ask another child to pick any of the remaining cards, again by pointing to it. Place this card in the same pile as the first card chosen. Remove all cards which were in the same row or column as the chosen card and discard them.

5.   Repeat the process twice more.

6.   Now ask a child to take the last card and put it with the four that were chosen and ask him/her to turn them over and rearrange the letters to form the name 'JESUS'.

7.   You can replace the cards as at 2 and let the children have another go. No matter which cards are chosen, they, together with the last card, will always comprise the five letters of the name 'JESUS'.

8.   Now tell the children that they can do this trick! Place the cards out for one child in the correct order, and ask him to do exactly as you did, by asking other children to pick the cards as in 3,4,5 & 6. See if the chosen cards form the name 'JESUS'.

9.   This can be repeated as many times as the children wish if they want to try and find out why it works.

Variation

The same trick may be done with any word, phrase or sentence, provided that the cards are laid out so that the word, phrase or sentence is repeated underneath the first line as many times as there are letters in it.

23

The same procedure as in 3 and 4 must be followed, and at 5, you repeat the process until only one card remains.

The chosen cards plus the remaining one will always form the original word, phrase or sentence.

A secret code of numbers may be put on the backs of the cards, so that they can be laid out by the leader without his having to look at the letters.

Discussion

It may be possible to lead into a discussion as follows:

In the game, the letters of JESUS were there even though we couldn't see them.

If we followed the instructions we realised that JESUS was always there.

In the game, we found JESUS, by following the advice of someone who wanted to show him to us.

Perhaps in life, we may find JESUS, a little more each day, by listening to, and being with, those who know he is with us always.

As in the Compass Points Game it may be helpful to read the last verses in Chapter 28 of St Matthew's Gospel. 'I am with you always.'—how can Jesus be, when we cannot see him? Will he keep his promise? The story of the Red Indian boy's initiation might be helpful here.

When he was to be a man he was taken deep into the forest as darkness fell and left alone through the night, with his fears and the noises of the forest night life, the dangers and the dark. And then as dawn came the boy would see that his father had kept vigil nearby, always there, always ready to protect his son in the face of danger.

Jesus, although we cannot see you we believe you are near. Help us to understand that you will always keep your promise to be with us.

Be with us to guide us:
Be with us to encourage us:
Be with us to strengthen us:
Be with us to love us.   Amen.

'Missions to Seamen' Game

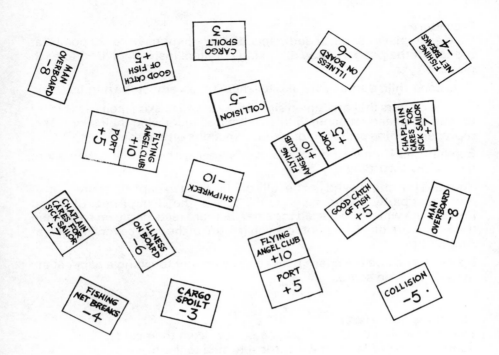

You will need

21 sheets of paper 10″ × 8″ (quarto size).

Small pieces of card, say 2″ × 1½″—one for each player.

Pencil and paper for each child to record his score (or you could use small plastic counters if you have enough to give 20 to each child at the start).

Preparation

Write the headings and + or − points values on the quarto sheets of paper as indicated in the above diagram.

Number the small pieces of card consecutively from 1, putting the number on both sides. If you like you can draw an outline picture of a ship on each side.

Lay out the quarto sheets on the floor in the middle of the room as shown in the above diagram.

Ask the players to form a circle round the layout of quarto sheets, each player to be at least 2 feet from the nearest sheet if space permits.

Procedure

Give each player a pencil and paper and tell them to write '20 points' at the top of the paper. (If you are using counters instead, give 20 to each player).

Give each child a small card and tell them to remember the number on it.

Tell the players that on a given signal they are all to skim their cards to try to land on sheets of paper with + values, so increasing their score. This represents ships sailing in different directions on the sea.

Explain that if they land on sheets of paper with − values, their score decreases accordingly.

The card (or 'ship') need not be fully on the sheet of paper to score + or −, it can rest partly on the paper. In the case of the Flying Angel Club and Port sheets which are placed together, if a card rests partly on each, then the Port score of +5 is counted, even if more of the card covers the Flying Angel Club.

If a card lands on the space between papers, not touching a paper at all, then there is no score.

The game now starts

The Leader shouts 'Go' and all the players skim their cards.
Scores are recorded and the cards returned to the players.

Play continues in this manner with rounds of skimming and recording scores.

Players are eliminated when their score falls to zero.

The game may be played over a fixed number of rounds, the player having the highest score at the end being the winner.

Alternatively, you can play until all players are eliminated except one— who is the winner. Or you can play to see who is the first to reach a certain number of points, say 40.

Discussion

This game could then lead into a discussion of the dangers and difficulties, the rewards and the pleasures of life at sea, bringing in the various aspects of the work of the 'Missions to Seamen'. The Leader would find it helpful to obtain some background literature from the Society for the discussion, and would need to be aware of the extent and depth to which the discussion could go, in relation to the ability of the children involved.

NB It may be necessary to use smaller sheets of paper for the floor layout if the room is small.

It may also be a good idea to sellotape the sheets to the floor if possible, to stop the cards from going underneath the sheets.

(This game was published in the 'Sea Sunday' packs for July 1976, issued by the Missions to Seamen.)

Variation
It would add colour to the game if simple line drawings could be put on the quarto sheets, appropriate to the incident indicated. Also, when a player lands on a quarto sheet, he could be given a small card which is a duplicate of the one he has landed on. This would help him to be more aware of the kinds of incidents which had helped him or hindered him in the game.

The Society issues many suitable prayers for use amongst all ages. The subject and game also lead very easily into 'write your own prayer'.

We tend to use words written for hymns only when we sing them! Why not use the following verse as the 'Together Prayer'?

> Eternal Father, strong to save,
> Whose arm doth guide the restless wave:
> Who bidd'st the mighty ocean deep
> Its own appointed limits keep!
> O hear us when we cry (pray) to Thee
> For those in peril on the sea. Amen.
> (For all who sail upon the sea)

(Bracketed words might be helpful alternatives.)

The Harvest Journey

Requirements
7 pieces of card about 7" square. On each one draw, preferably with a felt marker pen, one of the letters of the word HARVEST. Each letter should be quite large, as in the diagram below.

You will also need seven chairs on which you ask seven children to sit, all in a straight line facing the rest of the children.

You will need a blackboard or newsprint and a marker pen. Place the blackboard, (or the newsprint on a wall), so that the children on the straight line of chairs and the rest of the children can see it.

Beforehand, you will need to draw the diagram shown below, *without the words,* on the blackboard or the sheets of newsprint. Draw it large enough for the children to be able to see the words when they are written in the appropriate rectangles.

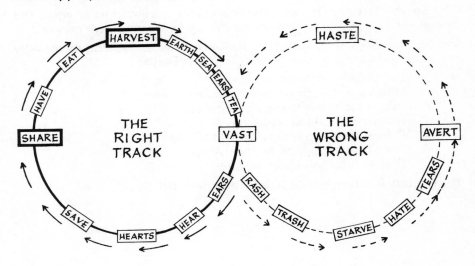

You are now ready to begin to tell the story of the Harvest Journey. The seven children should be sitting on the straight line of chairs, and the rest of the children should be able to see these children. All the children must be able to see the blackboard or sheets of newsprint.

The Harvest Journey

1. Ask the seven children who are sitting on the chairs to come forward and give each child one of the seven letter cards in random order. Now ask them to sit on the chairs holding the letter cards so that they face the rest of the children, and so that the word HARVEST is formed. Write this word in the top rectangle of the left-hand circle.

2. Now tell the children that we can make quite a number of words using the letters of the word HARVEST, and that some of these words will help us to remember parts of the Harvest Journey as it is related to them.

3. Ask the children to think of a word which can be made from the letters of the word HARVEST which they are looking at, which is the main source of all our vegetables and cereals and fruit, what are all of them grown in? When they offer the word EARTH, ask the children sitting on the chairs with the letters, to decide which letters are needed to form the word; then those holding the appropriate letters are to stand up, move forward slightly and rearrange themselves to form the word EARTH. You, or one of the other children, can now write the word EARTH in the rectangle next to the one containing the word HARVEST, moving in a clockwise direction. When the word has been written in the children standing with the letters can sit down in their original places so that the word HARVEST is again formed.

NB This is the procedure with each word which is highlighted in the story. You need to ask the right questions, and to give the children clues which lead them to the word you want. The children on the chairs then stand up and form the word with the appropriate letters, it is written in the appropriate rectangle, and the children sit down ready for the next word. With a bit of practice, you will be able to relate the Harvest Journey as a connected narrative.

4. Now ask them what is another source of much of the harvest. If necessary, bring in the idea of people going out in boats and ships—what do they catch? Fish—so what is another great source of our harvest? When the word SEA emerges, repeat the procedure in 3. above.

5. Remind them that we also have the harvest of industry, but there doesn't seem to be a word we can make from the available letters to help us. We get machines and equipment and materials from industry.

6. There are two words which help to remind us of the harvest of the earth. The first is to do with the . . . of corn; what is the missing word? What do we call the parts at the top of the stalk which hold the grain? When they get the word EARS repeat the procedure as before.

7. And the other word which reminds us of the harvest of the earth . . . it's to do with a drink. It's something which has to be picked and people are usually paid very poor wages for doing this . . . perhaps we should pay more for it—but only if we knew that the extra money would go to those

who were picking it. The word is TEA. Repeat procedure as before. (From now on, the appropriate word will be given in brackets at the end of each question.)

8.   Now explain that the population of the world is very, very large—now over 4,000,000,000. Also the harvest throughout the whole world is very large, in fact there is enough for us all. What is a word that means very, very large? This word can then help us to remember the size of the population and the size of the complete harvest throughout the whole world. (VAST)

9.   Now tell them that at this point we could go one of two ways on our journey—we could go on what could be the right track, or we could go on what may be the wrong track. Now write in the words as shown in the diagram: THE RIGHT TRACK and THE WRONG TRACK, and also put in the arrows.

10.   It may be helpful to explore the wrong track first so that it may help us to realise what may be a better track.

11.   If we don't think about what to do with the harvest, if some people grab most of it for themselves, and some people are left with very little, then there is a word which could describe our actions in grabbing too much. If they need another clue tell them that the same word is used to describe the spots we get in some diseases like measles! (RASH)

12.   What happens is some people take too much, and take the best of what is available from the harvest? What does this leave for others? (TRASH)

13.   If we take too much from the harvest, and leave too little for others, what will happen to them? What happens to people if they don't have enough food? They . . . . . . ? (STARVE)

14.   How do you think people who haven't got enough food feel about the people who they know are taking too much? One of the feelings they could have is . . . . (HATE)

15.   Also, if people are starving, and they are worried about their own lives and the lives of their children, there may be a lot of . . . around. What sometimes happened as a child when you felt you hadn't been given enough? Did you cry?—what happens when you cry? (TEARS)

16.   We seem to be on the wrong track. If we want to avoid people starving and hating and crying we must try a different track. What is another word which is similar in meaning to the word avoid? It starts with the same two letters. (AVERT)

17.   So we need to do things to avert or avoid this kind of misery and disaster. And we need to think things out carefully if we are to do this, but also we need to act quickly. What is a word which means quickness or speed? (HASTE)

18. Our actions in averting the disasters caused by some people having too much of the harvest and some having too little need to be done in some haste. So we return to the word VAST. Let's try to go off on a better track this time.

19. First we need to listen to what God is saying through Jesus, through God's Holy Spirit, and through other people, the rich, the poor, the affluent, the starving. What is he saying about our use of what he has given us in the harvest? If we are to listen we must use our . . . (EARS)

20. If we use our ears, and we really want to listen to what God is saying through other people, then we shall really . . . . (HEAR)

21. If we really hear, then we may believe in our . . . . . . how God wants us to use the harvest of the earth and the sea and industry, and the harvest of our minds. What word is missing? (HEARTS)

22. So there seem to be two things we need to think about and to do when we consider all these harvests. Instead of wasting precious food and water, and raw materials and the things we make from the raw materials, we need to learn to . . . . them. What is the opposite to wasting things? What verb can you get out of the letters of HARVEST which means to keep things instead of wasting them? Of course, in another way, if we can make sure that the harvest is distributed properly, then we can . . . . people from starving and from misery. The same word can be used again. (SAVE)

23. And now we come to what must be the most important word we can make from the word HARVEST. It means to distribute things fairly, if necessary, to give things to people, in order that those who have had too little of the harvest in the past may have more, and those who have had too much may learn to make do with less. We will put this word in a box with a thicker black line around it to emphasise it. What word comes to mind when you offer other people some of the things you have, when you let them play with your toys and games? (SHARE)

24. If we learn to share the harvest more fairly, then we may be able to save more people from starvation and misery. You may have heard the rich nations and the poor nations referred to as those who . . . . and those who . . . . not. What word is missing? (HAVE)

25. So if we learn to share some of what we have with those who have not, one benefit will be that we shall all have something to . . . What word could you put in there? If we are able to do this, we will not starve. What word are we after? (EAT)

26. So, at last, having learned to share our harvest more fairly, we can all, throughout the world, work with more of a feeling of hope and justice being involved in our efforts, and we can work towards producing another HARVEST.

27.   And now, looking at the diagram on the board, we can look back at the words we have been able to make from the seven letters of the word HARVEST. They remind us of the ways in which we can be on the wrong track in using God's gifts, and how we can help ourselves and others to get onto the right track—a track which is circular. It's a good circle. Whereas the other track, the wrong track, is a vicious circle, and if you are on that one everything can only get worse.

> We pray, dear Father God,
> To eat and not be hungry,
> To hear and not forget,
> To see and share the picture
> Of harvest through the world.
> You have given us a harvest
> From the land, the sea, the air,
> We are grateful, we will share it
> We will use it all with care.   Amen.

This Game offers many possible uses, interpretations and avenues of thought and activity. It is ideal for prayer making; for spontaneous prayerful response.

'Fish' Variations

This game is an adaptation of the card game 'Fish' which many children have played, in which a pack of playing cards is shuffled and laid face down on a flat surface. Each child in turn then has to turn over two cards. If they form a pair, e.g. two Aces, two fours, two Queens, then that player keeps the two cards, and has another go. When a player turns up two cards which are not a pair, he turns them back over and the next player has a go. Play continues until all the pairs have been found. The winner is the player with most pairs. Obviously this game depends a lot on memory.

However, it is possible to design packs of cards—the number of cards in a pack varies according to the number of pairs required. For instance, I once used it to help children to become acquainted with the Hebrew months of the year when we were doing a little course on the Jewish faith. I put the English months on 12 cards, and their approximate Hebrew equivalents on another set of 12 cards. Unfortunately, I didn't realise at the time that the card I used wasn't thick enough, and in some cases it was possible to guess what was written on a card. So don't fall into the same error!

Of course, I didn't really want the children to learn the Hebrew months of the year and their English equivalents so that they could repeat them parrot fashion—I can't see much point in things like that. On the other hand it provided an interesting game based on an aspect of the theme we were exploring.

One use of the game, suggested to me by John Harris-Douglas, was to use pairs of cards as follows:— one card would have on it a situation which Jesus was in as recorded in one of the accounts of the Gospel. The other card in the pair would have on it a saying of Jesus associated with that situation. An example is given below:—

Part of the prayer of Jesus, when he was in the Garden of Gethsemane on the night which we call Maundy Thursday night, was:—

'Father, if it be possible, let this cup pass from me. Nevertheless, not my will, but yours be done'.

The game now not only relies on memory, but also requires an awareness of the records of the gospel in order to play it.

You will of course, be able to think of your own pairs of situations and sayings, and this can be part of the fun of preparation.

The game can be adapted for use in any situation where pairs of names, places, objects, situations, etc., are relevant. You can, of course, at any stage, lay the cards out in pairs face up for the children to study, so that they have a better chance of playing the game, or you could let a small group of children sort them out into what they think are the correct pairs.

You could use pictures on one set and names on another, e.g. a picture of a chalice on one card and the word chalice on another.

We have to learn lots of things in life: all that we learn is stored in our memory. To succeed in this game we need to use our memory well. To succeed in life we need to use our memories well. Not only must we remember what are good things, what leads to success, but also we must remember the things in life which lead to hurt, to fault or failure. Have you noticed how difficult it is to remember everything accurately?

Thank you, God, for our memory, help us to use it well. We need to learn so much to be good workmen, good people, good followers of Jesus. Help us to remember what leads us in the wrong way and also what leads us in the right way.

Thank you, God, as well for a memory which helps us to have fun, to play games and to enjoy things.

Through Jesus Christ our Lord.   Amen.

Just Imagine!

God has given us the great gift of imagination. As we grow up most of us tend to use this gift less and less, whereas in childhood we probably had a vivid imagination, which we used in day-dreaming, painting pictures, writing stories, making models and playing with toys.

The exercise which follows is designed to stimulate the imagination. It has been used successfully with adults and teenagers as well as with children. On the next page is a reproduction of what we have called a 'splodge-print'. You will need one of these for each child and you can either make sufficient photo-copies of the one in this book, or use the method described at the end to make your own. (The method is simple and cheap but also rather messy. We have found that children enjoy making their own prints, so, having read how to make them, you may decide to take your courage in both hands and let them have a go!)

Procedure

1.   Give each child a pencil, a piece of paper, and either a photo-copy of the 'splodge-print' on the next page, or let them make their own—in which case you will need to allow extra time. (We have put some little grid marks round the sides of the print in this book to help identify the objects that we can see by using our imagination—you don't need to put these marks on if you make your own.)

2.   Explain to the children, in terms you feel they will understand, something about God's wonderful gift of imagination, how we use it and what fun we can have with it.

3.   Now ask them to look at the 'splodge-print' on p.36. They can look at it from any angle, they can turn it round in any direction. Look at the black shapes, the large and the very small, and the white shapes, large and small. Look at black and white shapes together. What sorts of things can they see? Ask them to make a list on the piece of paper. (Try to get the children to do this without any help—in other words, don't put ideas into their minds unless they really need them!) Try doing this exercise yourself at the same time as the children.

4.   If you notice that any child is stuck, you may like to point out what one or two shapes look like to you, carefully explaining that they may not look the same to him/her. For instance, can you see these shapes (the grid reference gives the approximate position on the 'splodge-print')? Notes at the side tell you which way to turn the page to look at the print.
  Horse lying on ground, head pointing up: From C to E between 2 and 3 (page upright). Poodle with bird sitting on head: From F to G between 2 and 3 (page upright). Duckling with beak pointing up: Between H and I and

11 and 12 (page upside down). Head and shoulders of a boxer aiming a punch: C8 (page upside down). Robin perched on a log: For between 8 and 9 (page ¼ turn anti-clockwise).

5.   When the lists are finished let the children form pairs and ask them to show each other the shapes they have seen. Can the partner also see the same shapes?—or is his imagination different in some cases?

6.   Now ask them to number the items on their lists without their partner seeing the numbering. Each child tells his partner how many items there are on his own list and the partner picks three numbers at random which are not greater than the number of items, thus choosing at random three things seen on the 'splodge-print'. Each child underlines the three chosen at random by his partner.

7.   Now ask each child to make up a short story, bringing in each of the three items on his own list which are underlined, and linking them together in some way so that they make an interesting story. The story should be about 500 words long.

8.   When the stories are finished (or when a time limit is up, say 20 minutes), let those children who would like to, read out their stories. (The story-writing/telling may be omitted if desired.)

9.   Ask the children if they can think of people who have used their imagination in a helpful way in life. What about artists, writers, scientists, musicians, toy-makers, parents?

10.   Now lead on to discuss ways in which the children themselves have used their imagination in life. What about drawing pictures, making up stories.

11.   Finish sharing ideas on how they think Jesus would like us to use our imagination in helping his church to be alive and welcoming.

How to make your own 'splodge-prints'

You will need a cardboard box, the bottom of which is just a bit bigger than a sheet of A4 or A5 or quarto duplicating paper.
Also a few sheets of A4 or A5 or quarto duplicating paper,
A discarded tube of duplicating ink and a piece of rag.
A large sheet (about 30" × 20") of good quality brown paper, shiny on one side.
A sheet of card slightly larger than the size of duplicating paper you are using.
A sharp 'lino-cutting' knife (Stanley knife) and some sellotape.

Procedure

1.   Cut the cardboard box about 3" from the bottom all the way round, discard the top part and retain the bottom 'tray'.

2.   Crumple up the brown paper and put it shiny side up into the tray so that it is all screwed up in the tray.

3.   Make a pad of the rag and smear it with duplicating ink and dab the brown paper in the tray until most of it has some duplicating ink on.

4.   Fasten a sheet of duplicating paper to the sheet of card with sellotape at the corners.

5.   Place the sheet of card with the duplicating paper face *down* in the tray and press hard—do not move it from side to side, try to keep the card in that position as you press it.

6.   Remove the sheet of card which should now have a 'splodge-print' on the duplicating paper. Remove the print carefully and let it dry. Repeat with more sheets of duplicating paper and let them dry. Choose the ones which you think are best.

7.   Carefully wrap everything else up in newspaper and put in the dustbin before you get black ink marks everywhere!

Dear God,
   We thank you for the wonderful gift of imagination. We can enjoy imagining people, places and happenings, but truly we need our imagination too.

We need to imagine what life must have been like for Jesus. We need to imagine what life is like for other people, for people whom we . . .
   (mention your special interest e.g. those who are lonely or hungry, those who have achieved something wonderful, etc.)

When we are young, help us to help older people to use their imagination too, for as we all grow older we seem to find it more difficult to be imaginative.

Thank you, God, for our imagination.
                              Amen.
(When there is a long prayer it may be more helpful to use only a section of it.)

That's not what I meant!

In hundreds of different ways throughout life, we have to try to explain to other people what we mean, what we have seen or heard, or how we feel. In an age of mass communication through radio, TV, telephones, newspapers and the like, we still have problems in communicating with each other.

No wonder then that we have problems in trying to help other people to understand something about God, Jesus Christ, the Holy Spirit, the Gospel, the Church. First, *we* need to have some understanding and that isn't easy to come by! Then we need to find helpful ways of sharing some of our understanding—realising that it will be mixed up with a lot of our misunderstanding as well.

So perhaps we need to think a little more about how we make mistakes in communicating things to each other. There's the other half of it as well—how do we listen to what people are trying to get over to us? Do we hear something quite different from what was meant?

This little exercise is designed to make us more aware of some of the basic difficulties of communication.

You will need several different line drawings—one drawing per sheet of A5 or quarto paper—similar to the ones shown below. Each drawing should be backed with a piece of cardboard so that it is impossible to see through from the back. (If you have 12 children you will need half that number of line drawings, i.e. 6.)

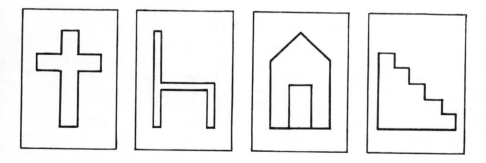

The suggested shapes are from left to right, a cross, chair, dog-kennel and stone steps.

Procedure
1. Pair the children off. They then sit down in pairs as widely separated

as the room will allow. Half the pairs are to sit facing each other, the other half back to back.

2.   Give one child in each pair a pencil and a piece of paper the same size as that used for the line drawings, and a board or book on which to rest the paper.

3.   Give the other child in each pair a line drawing. Take care that the children who have paper and pencil do not see the line drawings.

4.   Now explain that the children who have the line drawings are to try to describe them so that their partner can draw them but with the following limitations about the description:—

(a)   They can describe *where a line starts* from by saying 'put a dot 5 cms. from the bottom of the paper and 3 cms. from the right hand edge.', and where it finishes by the same method and tell their partner to join the two dots.

(b)   They can tell them the *length* of a line.

(c)   They can tell them the *direction,* e.g. up, down, to the left, to the right, diagonally up the left etc.

(d)   They must *not* describe the object in any way, or say it is similar to anything else (e.g. they must not say 'like a letter h' in the case of the chair).

(e)   They must not describe the shape of any part of an object (e.g. they musn't say 'rectangle', 'square', 'triangle' etc.).

To sum up they can only describe:—where a line starts
where a line finishes
how long a line is
what direction a line goes in

(f)   No questions allowed. Only one repeat of an instruction.

5.   Allow about 5 minutes for the description and drawing. Then let those who have been drawing look at the line drawings held by their partner. Tell them to do this with as much secrecy as possible so that other children do not see the line drawing they have been using. Ask them to discuss quietly any problems they had in describing or drawing.

6.   Collect the line drawings and the other drawings with as much secrecy as possible and give pencil and paper to those who were the 'describers' last time. Now give the other child in each pair a line drawing. Make sure that it isn't the same as the one they have just tried to draw.

7.   Allow 5 minutes for description and drawing again, followed by discussion of any problems in pairs.

8.   Come together as a group. Share any problems which were experienced. Did the ones who were back to back miss the chance to make facial expressions, i.e. communicate with a nod, a frown, etc?

9.   What problems do the children think Jesus had in helping people to understand something about God, his Father and his Kingdom? What ways did Jesus use to try to make it easier for people to understand? How did he try to make it easier for people to learn how to get on with each other and with God? How did he try to make it easier for us to understand how to use the good things which God has given us, like food, clothing, shelter, time, abilities?

O God,
    Help us to say and show
        what we mean
    And to mean what
        we say and show

    To be sorry if we are not clear
    and to forgive if we are
    misunderstood.

    Thank you, Jesus, for
        saying and showing us
        so clearly what our
        Heavenly Father is like
        and how he would
        have us live.
                Amen.

Picture Matching

This is mainly for younger children, although by using harder correlations, older ones could benefit from the exercise.

As in Fish Variations (No. 9), you need two sets of correlated cards. In this case, however, you need one set made up of larger pictures—about A5 or A4 size—and these are stuck on the walls at various points round the room.

You then give each child one card from the other set, on which there is a word or phrase (to help younger children and slow readers, you could add corresponding pictures), and ask them to go and find the appropriate picture on the wall and stand by it.

Ask the children in turn, why they chose the picture by which they are now standing. If some children have chosen wrongly, help them to work out the correct 'pairing'. You could ask them what sorts of things they like about the picture they are next to. Or perhaps there are things they dislike?

When that round of 'pairing' and discussion has finished, collect the small cards which they are holding, shuffle them, and deal them out again. Ask the children to find the appropriate picture again, and repeat the procedure in the last paragraph.

If you wish you can have further rounds, until most of the children have paired off most of the small cards with the large pictures.

An alternative is to put up a set of the pictures produced by the Benedictine Nuns of Cockfosters and published by Nelson—the ones about the Teaching of Jesus, or the Parables of Jesus.

In this case, give each child a Bible reference. The references could be written on small pieces of paper beforehand, so that they can be dealt with out to the children. They then have to look up the reference in a Bible and locate the picture to which it refers. As described above, you could ask the children why they chose the picture—why did they believe it related to the Bible reference which they were given? What sorts of things do they like or dislike about their picture?

Again, the references could be collected in, shuffled, and dealt out afresh.

Afterwards, you could ask the children to go and stand by the picture which they like best, or by the one which they feel tells us most about caring for others.

For drawings that tell us a story;
For paintings that show us your glory;
For artists and printers,
For pictures which teach us,
We thank you, Dear Father
Our God.   Amen.

The Tour of Knowledge

General outline
You will need 15 Question Sheets stuck on the wall—at the children's eye level—at intervals round the room. Each child will need a Tour Card and a pen or pencil.

Requirements
The basic layout of the Question Sheets is as in the diagram—try using A4 sheets of paper and a felt pen.

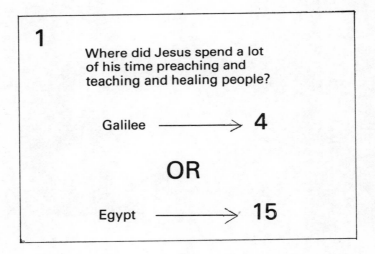

The number of the Question Sheet appears in the top left hand corner. Two alternative answers are given to each question, one being correct, the other incorrect. The arrow following each answer points to a number—this tells participants which Question Sheet to go on to next. For example, if you felt that Galilee was the correct answer—see diagram—you would go on to Question Sheet 4. If, however, you felt that Egypt was the correct answer, you would proceed to Question Sheet 15.

You can make up your own set of 15 questions, each with two alternative answers, on any subject you like—they needn't be based solely on the bible.

The sequence of numbers which you put on the 15 Question Sheets is as follows:

Question Sheet No.	Correct Answer to:	Incorrect Answer to:
1	4	15
2	7	3
3	9	8
4	13	5
5	1	11
6	12	5
7	15	8
8	5	14
9	14	8
10	2	11
11	6	15
12	8	11
13	10	14
14	11	3
15	3	5

Important
You must vary the position of the correct answer from sheet to sheet, so that on some sheets it is the uppermost answer and on the other sheets it is the lower one.

Tour Cards
You will need as many Tour Cards as there are children playing the game. They should look like the one in the diagram.

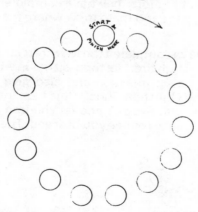

If you have 15 children or less, prepare 15 Tour Cards and number them from 1–15 in the circle marked 'Start and finish here'.

If you have between 16 and 30 children number two sets of Tour Cards from 1–15.

Procedure

Tell the children that you have put 15 Question Sheets on the walls around the room, and that they are numbered 1–15 in the top left hand corner and are in order so that they are easy to find. Explain that each Question Sheet has a question on it, with two alternative answers, one is correct and the other is wrong, and that there is an arrow from each answer pointing to a number. That number tells them which Question sheet to proceed to next if they choose that answer as the correct one.

Now shuffle the Tour Cards and give one to each child together with a pen or pencil.

Tell them that they are to start at the Question Sheet indicated in the 'Start and finish here' circle on their Tour Card. (As you are using one or two sets of Tour Cards numbered 1–15, depending on the number of children taking part, the children will be distributed evenly round the Question Sheets at the start). Also explain that when they start at the Question Sheet indicated on their Tour Card, they are to decide which they think is the correct answer, make a note of the next Question Sheet they have been directed to in the next small circle on their Tour Card and proceed to that Sheet and repeat the same procedure.

Tell them that if they answer every one of the 15 questions correctly they will find that they have visited each of the 15 Question Sheets once and once only, and that they will return to the Question Sheet they first started at on their fifteenth move. Explain that if they answer one or more questions incorrectly they will find that they return to a Question Sheet they have already been to before they have completed the 'tour'. If that happens, they must go back and try to think where they may have gone wrong and try again.

When all the children have completed the tour correctly, or when you feel you have given them enough time, let them sit down while you give them the correct answers to each question and also give them the correct sequence of visits to the Question Sheets. It is best to follow the correct tour through from Question Sheet 1 and let children who have started from other Sheets pick up the tour as you proceed. The correct sequence is indicated below.

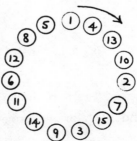

46

Any children who didn't complete the tour correctly, may now like to go round again to gain the satisfaction of knowing that it is possible.

Discussion

Playing the Tour of Knowledge game is an excellent way of opening up a discussion about the subject matter contained in the questions. Discussion may take place while you are giving them the answers to the questions, or you may like to keep the discussion period until after you have shown them the correct sequence for the tour. Either way, you should find that even though the Tour of Knowledge game has to be based on facts in order to have correct and incorrect answers, the playing of it will provoke a discussion where opinions and attitudes about the subject matter have a chance to be aired.

General Notes

You may like to ask children to go round in pairs with one Tour Card per pair so that they can discuss the questions and answers as they try to complete the tour. You can also range the wrong answers through from the nearly correct to the absurd.

This Tour of Knowledge game idea has been used with groups of adults and young people to stimulate interest and discussion about Industrial Relations. The European Community, Synodical Government, 'The Child in the Church' Report and other issues, so do feel free to experiment with the content of the Question Sheets.

It is fun to say, 'I know.'
It is good to say, 'I think I know.'
It is essential to say, 'God help me to know—what is right.'

> We thank you God for:
> the knowledge which comes from
> people of the past:
> the knowledge which is being
> discovered now:
> the knowledge which you will show us
> through the guidance
> of your Holy Spirit,
> Through Jesus Christ Our Lord.
> Amen.

Acknowledgement

Waddingtons Quiz Card Games are based on the Tour of Knowledge idea devised by Michael Kindred and Malcolm Goldsmith. Waddingtons Playing Card Co. Ltd., of Leeds, have kindly given permission for the idea to be used in its original form in this book.

Search Quiz

This can be used to teach a complete new set of facts, or for revision, or for a mixture of both.

The participants need to be told that this quiz game is to be played in a co-operative way, so that they don't feel that they have to compete with one another.

1. Prepare a quiz containing as many questions as there are children in the group.

In preparing the questions and answers, you need to bear in mind that the answers could be:

(a) all of the same kind, e.g. all numbers, or all names of rivers. This makes it harder for the participants to pair off the answers with the questions.

(b) made up of some of one kind, some of another, and some of another. e.g. some could be names of famous people, some names of trees, some, names of birds.

(c) all different, e.g. if one question was 'Who discovered penicillin?', there would be only one answer in the quiz which was the name of a person. This makes it easier for the participants to pair off the answers with the questions.

2. Duplicate a set of questions—with space for children to write in the answers—for each child.

3. Write each answer out on a separate small card.

4. Give a set of questions, a pencil, and one of the answer cards to each child.

5. Each child now has to mingle with all the others in the group and 'swap' answers. Answers are 'swapped' by the showing of cards to each other, not by exchanging them, so that each child retains the same answer card throughout the quiz game. Each child has to write down the answers against the appropriate questions as the 'swapping' proceeds.

6. Although this is a game of co-operation, it is necessary to tell the children not to show each other their partly completed questions sheets at any stage during the game, as this would defeat one of the objects of the game from the learning and revising point of view.

An alternative to 5 is to ask the children to mingle and find out the names of the children who have the answers. In this case, the appropriate name is written in the answer space. In this way the Search Quiz can also help members of a new group to get to know one another.

NB   The questions and answers could be based on the person and character of Jesus, or places in the New Testament, or Festivals of the Church, etc.

New facts have to be learnt each day. Perhaps a day when we learn nothing new is a wasted day! Do you think so?

Revision is also important: and not just before a test or exam.

We learn about God's world, we learn about his people. We need to think again about this knowledge, to revise our learning.

> Thank you God for learning.
> Help us to enjoy new facts and
> to enjoy revising
>   The time we spend on learning
> is your time: thank you for our
> time of learning.
>   Amen.

It's a Piece of Cake!

This idea can be used to teach new material. The enjoyment of solving
the puzzle enhances the learning. The questions and answers can be
based on various aspects of the Christian Faith. A sample set of questions
and answers is given on the diagram.

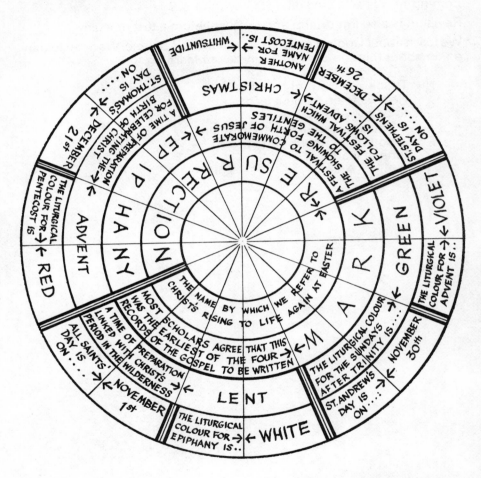

Mark out the above diagram on a piece of card. If your questions and
answers are more wordy than the ones shown, you will need to enlarge
the drawing. The size shown, or slightly larger is suitable for an individual
to use. For group use, it should be drawn about twice the size.

You will need a set of 15 questions and answers. 8 will be written in the outer ring, 4 in the next ring, 2 in the next one, and 1 in the inner ring.

Now cut the completed 'cake' out of the piece of card, and then cut the 'cake' into the 16 segments.

For individual use: The problem is to reassemble the cake.

For a group of 16 participants: give each member a segment. Let them mix freely around the room. Explain that each player has a question or an answer in the outer band of his piece of cake. He must try to find the player with the appropriate answer or question on his outer band. When the two pieces are put together, a question or answer will appear in the next band. These two players must then try to find the two players who have the appropriate answer or question in the next band on their pair of segments, and so on, until the cake is reassembled. Members hold on to their segments until the whole group is standing in the right order. The whole 'cake' can then be placed on a table.

There are many sorts of cake: chocolate, cream or jammy sponge, ginger or window-cake, rich fruit or currant-buns.

Lots of ingredients go to make these cakes and cooks must learn which ones; they must learn how to mix and bake or ice or decorate. Thank you, Lord, for cakes—and cooks.

There are lots of types of Christian life, great, small or in-between. There are facts to learn, ideas to try and deeds we can perform.

Mixture
Lord Jesus help us, as we pray,
To learn more about you, and more of our friends.
To care for God's world, his creatures, and use
this time for each other, your work and his glory.
Help us, Lord Jesus, each day.

Amen.

THETA Trading Game

THETA is an educational trading game which enables the participants to experience some aspects of:—

> greed and generosity
> selfishness and concern for others
> injustice and justice
> power and love
> competition and co-operation

The leader should look for instances of the above responses and their absence during the playing of the game so that he can refer to them in the discussion.

Age Range
This game has been used with children of secondary school age, older teenagers and adults.

Number of participants
Minimum 10—maximum 16

Room Layout
3 small tables with sufficient chairs grouped round each table. Each group to be as far away from the other two as space permits.

For the discussions, sheets of newsprint on the wall are helpful.

Time required
For the actual game—between 20 and 30 minutes.

For the ensuing discussion—10 to 30 minutes, depending on those who are taking part.

Leader's preparation
In addition to the preparation of the materials, etc., required for the game which are listed further on, the leader should be well acquainted with how the game is to be run, and must be aware of the kinds of reactions and responses for which he should be looking. He may also like to prepare a list of questions and discussion points to supplement those given at the end of the game description. These, together with his

observations of the reactions and responses during the game, should enable him to maintain a lively discussion.

The responses listed at the beginning may be related to the following:—
1. Family life—father, mother, brother, sister relationships.
2. The school environment.
3. The church and its work in the community.
4. National economic problems.
5. Relationships between the rich nations and the Third World.

The discussions should be aimed at starting from the participants' own experiences in the game and in their lives, and leading them on in their own terms to some understanding of the effects of greed, selfishness, power, etc., on others, and to some realisation of how these effects may be counteracted by generosity, co-operation, love, etc. It must be emphasised that good preparation by the leader is essential, to enable him to lead the discussions sensitively, thereby being aware of the depth to which the participants can, and cannot go.

Requirements

1. 16 Yellow cards, say 3" × 2" with WHEAT written on in large letters.
   16 Blue cards, same size with   MEAT   "   "   "   "   "
   16 Red cards, same size with   VEG   "   "   "   "   "

These are the numbers of cards to use if there are 16 participants. If there are less participants, reduce the number of each colour of card accordingly.

2. 'Pretend' money to the value of 4,500. Try to borrow some of this kind of paper money from one of the popular board games. Make sure that you have enough of the smaller denominations of notes so that change can be given in the trading sessions.

3. Divide the cards and money as follows and put in three different envelopes which should be sealed:—

For 16 participants

*ALPHA	: WHEAT	8	: MEAT	9	: VEG	5 Money	2,200
*BETA	: "	6	"	4	" 9	"	1,500
*GAMMA:	"	2	"	3	" 2	"	800
		16		16	16		

For 10 participants

WHEAT	6	: MEAT	7	: VEG	3
"	3	"	2	"	5
"	1	"	1	"	2
	10		10		10

* Write these names on the appropriate envelopes.

NB   The allocation of the money remains the same regardless of the number of participants. The allocation of the coloured cards for more than 10 participants and less than 16 should be worked out in roughly the same proportions as the two examples above. The total number of cards used for each commodity must be the same as the number of participants in the whole group.

4.   Small cards with ALPHA, BETA or GAMMA on them, depending on the number of participants as follows:—

Number of participants:—	Number of cards with the name on:—		
	ALPHA	BETA	GAMMA
10	2	3	5
11	2	3	6
12	2	4	6
13	2	4	7
14	2	4	8
15	2	5	8
16	3	5	8

5.   Paper and pencils for recording the trading results.

Procedure   (The participants should sit in a circle or 'horseshoe' at the start)

1.   Explain that for the purpose of this game, they are to imagine that they are the inhabitants of some islands in the middle of the ocean. These islands are called ALPHA, BETA, and GAMMA. Tell them that you are going to give each person a card which will show them to which island they belong.

2.   Shuffle the name cards and deal one to each person, face down.

3.   Tell them which table represents which island and ask them to sit at the appropriate table. The number of participants at each table represents the number of people on each island.

4.   Give a pencil and a sheet of paper to each island.

5.   Give out the appropriate sealed envelope to each island, ask them to open it and *quietly* see what the contents are, so that islands are not aware of what each other has received.

6.   Explain that this is a trading game. Tell them that each coloured card represents enough of the food described on it to feed one person for a year. Tell them that the 'money' is for use in trading with the other islands, and that each person needs wheat and meat and vegetables to survive each year.

54

7. Ask each island to elect a trading representative. Allow one minute for this.

8. Explain that during the first trading session, you want the representatives to take some money or goods with them and go in their 'Boat'—(Each island has a boat for ferrying representatives and goods)—and try to buy or sell food on the other two islands. *The aim is to do the best trading possible.* If they ask what you mean by 'the best trading possible' tell them they are to work that out for themselves during the playing of the game.

9. *First Trading Session*—there are two minutes in which to trade. The reps. may visit either or both of the other two islands in whatever order they prefer. It is helpful if the leader warns when only 30 seconds are left.

10. Reps. return to their own islands at the end of the trading session.

11. Ask each island to add up how many of each card they now have, and how much money. Go round each island in turn and make a note of these quantities and amounts. Try to do this so that the other islands are not aware of the figures.

12. *Second Trading Session*—(different representatives may be elected) there are two minutes in which to trade—the leader should once again emphasise that the aim is to do the best trading possible.

13. Repeat the procedure at 10 and 11.

14. Now ask each island to prepare a 'world broadcast' about the state of their island with regard to food and money. Have they enough of each kind of food for each person for a year? Have they too much or too little? Have they plenty of money or very little? Is anyone going to be under-nourished? Is anyone going to starve? The 'text' of the broadcast should be written down on a piece of paper, and should take about one minute to broadcast.

15. Ask each island in turn to send a broadcaster to the middle of the room to make the broadcast about the state of their island.

16. *Third Trading Session*—(different reps. may be chosen)
Again there are two minutes in which to trade.

17. Repeat the procedure at 10 and 11.

18. Have a *Fourth Trading Session.*
Repeat the procedure at 10 and 11.

19. Form everyone into a horseshoe arrangement for the discussion.

20. Write down on the sheets of newsprint, the amounts of food and money each island had at the beginning and after each trading session.

Discussion

1.   Ask them if they have any comments about the allocation of money and food at the start.

2.   Ask them how they felt about the inequality of the numbers of people on each island.

3.   How did they trade at the beginning? What basis did they use. How did they decide what to charge for the different food items?

4.   What did they think was meant by being asked to do the best trading possible?

5.   Ask them what they think would have happened if they had continued to have further periods of trading. Would those with plenty of food and money become complacent? Would those with not much food and money become irritated or bored?

6.   How did they feel about the broadcasts of other islands? How did they respond? How true was the picture presented in each broadcast? Did islands disguise figures and facts given to benefit themselves?

7.   Are there any helpful comments that can be made about the way the distribution of food and money changed during the game? What happened to the rates of exchange—the prices being charged for food—did inflation take hold?

8.   As leader, you probably heard various comments during the trading sessions, and at other times. Mention some of these and ask for their comments.

9.   Ask them what they thought the game may have been about. Was it just a game? Or was it a game which—however over-simplified—(as most simulations have to be) helped to simulate something to do with relationships and stewardship? Can we learn anything from our responses in the game which will throw some light on how we relate and fail to relate to each other at home, at school, at work? Does it have any bearing on our national economic problems, or on our relationships with the poorer countries? Do the rich get richer and the poor get poorer?

10.   Does the game have any bearing on the moral problems of inflation and rates of inflation?

11.   What are some of the difficulties and the joys involved in caring and sharing?

12.   How could the participants in the game have made sure that the food and money were more fairly distributed? Is there a difference between needs and wants? What about fairer rules for trading? What about giving away what we do not really need?

13.   Finally, you may like to consider the five pairs of responses to situations listed at the beginning of the general outline. What happens in

relationships when one person is being greedy or selfish, wielding power, being unjust, trying to compete? How are relationships deepened and improved by generosity, concern for others, by a right and proper love of yourself and others, by justice and co-operation?

The leader will need to use his own judgment in deciding when to close the discussion.

N.B.   If you can obtain the use of two or three interconnecting rooms so that the islands can be further apart and possibly out of sight of each other, then the playing of the game is easier. If you are lucky enough to have such facilities, you will need to explain as much as you can about the game while the participants are all together as a group, before you send them to their respective islands. For the 'broadcasts', you would need to bring the three islands together during them.

> Dear God,
>   Help us to be generous
>   and not greedy,
>   to share and not to grab.
>   Help us to think of others
>   and not to be selfish or unkind.
>   Help us to be just and true,
>   to think less of me and
>   more of you.
>   Amen.

Each aspect of the Game could be a theme for children's own prayers; indeed each lesson learned needs to be summed-up or expressed in prayer.

OMEGA Stewardship Game

Requirements

1. 3 identical sets of 12 different advertisements by charitable organisations. These may be cut out of newspapers and periodicals.

2. 3 pieces of paper, say 4" × 3". On one piece write £10, on the next write £40, and on the third write £120. Fold each piece of paper in two.

3. Paper and pencil for each group.

Procedure

1. Divide into unequal groups according to the number of participants, as outlined in the THETA Trading Game.

2. Give a set of charity adverts to each group.

3. Give the smallest group the piece of paper with £120 on it, the medium-size group the one with £40 on it, and the largest group the one with £10 on it.

4. Tell them that each group has the amount of money shown on their piece of paper to give to charitable causes. The twelve causes available are the ones shown on the adverts.

5. Ask them to spend about 10 minutes coming to a common decision in each group as to how they wish to allocate their amount of money. Tell them to write down how they have decided to allocate the money. They may give the money to one, some or all of the charities available.

6. Now ask each group to elect a representative. These representatives will now meet for three minutes to decide whether the charities concerned would be helped in a better way if they met as one large group and pooled their resources.

7a. If they decide to do this, ask them to form into one large circle, and work out as a group, how they would now like to re-allocate their giving. Allow ten minutes or so for this. Ask one member to write down the final results.

OR

7b. If, at 6, they decide not to meet together as a group, ask the representatives to go back to their own groups and report what happened at the meeting. Allow two or three minutes for this.

8. Form the group into a horseshoe arrangement, and write the results of the first allocation on the sheets of newsprint, and the revised allocation if they all met together as a group.

Discussion

1. Ask them how they felt when they realised that each group had different amounts of money to give away.

2. What basis, methods, did they use to make the initial allocation? Were some charities more 'popular' than others? Did some get ignored or forgotten? Why?

3. Were all the amounts allocated worth giving or were some small enough to involve a charity in more administration than it was worth?

4. If you did 7a, did the re-allocation, and the pooling of resources, help the overall giving?

5. Did anyone feel that there were charitable concerns that should have been included in the adverts? Did they feel that any of the adverts should have been excluded?

6. What sorts of considerations, feelings, etc., are involved in 'giving'? What about giving time and abilities, as well as money? Is concern for others only about giving money? Should we be helping the less fortunate to help themselves?

Is it easier to give or to receive?

How do we feel when doing both?

Each 'charity' or giving or receiving situation demands its own prayer.

Perhaps such a prayer needs to reflect our feelings.

Each prayer could be started by:

      Dear Father God,

         Help us to feel right in giving and receiving: ....

             . . . .

                                      Amen.

Planning a Town

This simulation may be used to help the participants to be aware of what happens in group decision-making situations. It is suitable for the 11–15 age range, older teenagers and adults.

It can be used with a single group of up to 12 people or 3 or 4 separate groups each having their own town planning set.

General Procedure

1.   Two large sheets of paper—newsprint or similar—about 30" × 20" each, are pinned or taped side by side and a map similar to the one in the diagram is drawn on it.

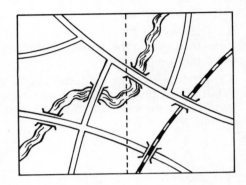

Basically, there need to be two through roads and three branch roads, plus a railway and a stream.

2.   On a piece of coloured card—say 20" × 12"—draw 1" squares on it lightly in pencil. Buildings of different shapes and sizes are drawn on this grid and then cut out. The following is a basic list to which you may add if you want to: Houses, flats, shops, supermarket, railway station, bus station, library, school, doctor's surgery, Police Station, Ambulance station, Fire station, Church, cinema, offices, public houses, sewage works, Hospital, engineering factory. These should be clearly labelled with a marker pen to show what they represent. A pair of houses could occupy 2 squares, blocks of flats may be 3 × 2 squares, the school may be 4" × 3 squares etc. As long as there is an appropriate idea of size for each building relative to the map, then this is sufficient.

3.   If you want to spread this exercise over two weeks or more, the players could make models of the buildings—given the area each building has to cover as indicated in 2 above.

4.   The 'buildings' are then placed round the edge of the map.

5.   A maximum of 12 players sit round the map in a circle.

6.   The leader explains that they are going to plan a town, using the roads, railway and stream that are already there on the map.

7.   He then asks a player to go to the board, select a building, and place it on the map in what he/she feels is the best position.

8.   Players then take it in turn round the circle to choose a building and place it on the map. (Notice the choice of buildings!)

9.   When all the buildings have been placed on the map, ask the players what they think about the layout and the planning. Which buildings do they think are in good positions—which badly placed? (e.g. Is the sewage works next to the supermarket?—is the police station next to the pub?).

10.   Now ask the players if they have any comments about the way you asked them to plan the town. Did it work just to have players taking a building in order and putting it where they liked on the map! Each person was forced to put his building on in relation to the buildings already there—or he could choose to ignore them.

11.   Ask them how they might be able to produce a better plan.

12.   If they come up with any practical ideas, try them out.

13.   If not, suggest that they split into three or four groups where they can see the map and buildings, give the leader in each group a paper and pencil and let them try to work out a better plan.

14.   Each group then demonstrates its plan and hears the criticisms of the rest of the players.

15.   Help the players to discuss the merits or otherwise of each plan.

16.   Remind them that buildings represent in a practical form the varying needs and wants of the people who together form the larger units in society.

17.   Help them to realise that they have been given very little information on which to base their planning. Try to lead on to a more general discussion about how we make decisions in groups. Leadership, co-operation, disunity, etc. are all topics that may be brought into the discussion.

18.   This could lead on to a discussion of how Jesus and his disciples worked as a group—and how the disciples worked after the Resurrection.

NB   In 2. above it was suggested that you may wish to add to the basic list of buildings which was given. Further suggestions are:—A nursery, an old people's home, A youth club, A health clinic, A job centre, Social Security offices.
       If you find that as a group you can't fit all the buildings onto the map, how do you each feel about the buildings that have been included and the ones that have been left out? What kinds of factors influenced the choices?

Sometimes it is easy to work with other people, often it is hard. Some groups find it difficult to plan a town, others find it easy.

It is also often difficult to remember the needs of every group of people and even more difficult to meet these needs.

We are called on to work with others and to be aware of their needs in this and every situation.

O God,

Whose loving design gave the world in trust to man, help all who organise and plan for the needs of the people in our village (town, city, community).

Help us all to be aware of each other's needs and to be willing to work for the common good.

Through Christ our Lord. Amen.

Planning a Worship Area

1. Make two cards 8cm × 4cm using coloured card—a fairly strong orange or red is a good colour to use.

On one of the cards write the following with a felt-tip pen:—

'The Presence of Jesus in the Bread and Wine'

On the other card write the following:—

'The Glory of Jesus shown by Musical Instruments'

2. Make 3 cards 4cm square using the same coloured card.

On one card put:—   'Jesus in the Word'
On another put:—   'Jesus made known to us through the Preacher'
On the third put:—   'The welcome of Jesus through Baptism'

3. Make sixty plain cards 4cm square using a different coloured card—say light blue.

4. Make forty cards 3cm square using a different coloured card—say yellow.

Put one of the following descriptions on each card:— (Choose from the 45 given)

A crippled woman	A 'show-off' little boy	An elderly choirman
A female churchwarden	A young girl	A priest on holiday
A male churchwarden	A young boy	An elderly choirlady
A young choirboy	A churchwarden's daughter	A churchwarden's son
An elderly deaf man	A teenage choirboy	A young woman
A mother with baby	An elderly woman	A young blind woman
A Jamaican woman	a black child	A woman recently bereaved
A baby in a pram	The churchwarden's husband	The churchwarden's wife
A shy little boy	A quiet teenager	A young mother
A young choirgirl	A giggly choirgirl	A noisy choirboy
A crippled man	A deaf woman	A young man
An elderly man	A noisy girl	A shy little girl
A toddler	The 'Pillar of the Church'!	A fidgety choirboy
A shy choirgirl	A noisy young boy	A middle-aged woman
A middle-aged man	A tramp	An Asian man

5. Give the five orange (or red) cards and the sixty plain light blue cards to a group of not more than six children. Tell them that the sixty plain cards represent a piece of furniture large enough for one person to sit on in the worship area of a church or other building which has a space set aside for worship. Explain that the orange (or red) cards are meant to

represent the places in a worship area where special and important activities occur. (The descriptions on each of these five cards represent an attempt to avoid the use of the words: altar, font, lectern, pulpit, organ, so that the natural creativity of the children is not stifled too much).

6.   Now ask them as a group to try to work together on planning out a worship area. Naturally, there will be different ideas and attitudes in the group, but they are to try to resolve these so that they can come to a common mind on one layout. Allow 15 to 20 minutes for this. (They will need a flat working surface so that they can move the cards around easily).

7.   Now give the group the small yellow cards and tell them to share these cards fairly equally between the members of the group. When they have done this, each member of the group takes one of his/her yellow cards and tries to imagine that they are the person described on the card and that they are coming into the worship area to sit down. Where would they sit? When they have decided they place their yellow card on the appropriate blue one and the next member of the group has a turn.

8.   When all the yellow cards have been placed on blue cards, the group should be given the chance, in silence, to contemplate the layout they have prepared.

9.   The leader can now initiate a discussion based on two aspects of the exercise:—

   (a)   How do members of the group feel about the layout? Why did they arrange the orange cards in the way they have done? Why do they feel that their seating arrangement is a good one? Were there any minority views in the group on any aspect of the planning?

   (b)   How did the group approach the task as far as decision-making was concerned? Did anyone dominate the group? Did anyone feel left out? Did a 'leader' emerge naturally? Did anyone try to oppose any leadership which emerged? Did this lead to a tendency for the group to split and become disunited?

10.   The discussion could lead on to how we see our role as a church in welcoming each other and welcoming new people. What sort of community do we offer to people on the fringe who may be wondering whether to become more involved? Is there any feeling of continuity in being members of the Body of Christ—do babies, toddlers, young children, older children, teenagers, young men and women, older men and women, and the elderly feel related to one another and accepted— and how is this expressed in the worship area and in the worship?

N.B.   If you were to make two or more sets of the cards, you could involve more than one group. Groups could then look at each other's layouts and comment on them and ask questions about them.

O God,
      We come together to worship you,
      To sing your praises,
      To hear your word.
      We come to think about you
      and about your world.
      We come together to pray for others
      as well as for ourselves.
      We come together to remind ourselves
      that Jesus is with us at all times.
      May he strengthen us to go out
      into the World to tell the world of
      your love and to show your glory.
      Through Jesus Christ our Lord.
          Amen.

'The Jigsaw of Life'

Each day of our lives new experiences come to us; information, sights and sounds, pour in upon child and adult alike. An ongoing task is to fit them into existing patterns, co-ordinating and making 'wholes'.

The making of the jigsaw helps children of any age to see how new knowledge fits with old, how life builds up into a picture. By doing this with experiences of the world about them, and from their own lives, they may make sense more easily of other 'life areas' in which we want them to share, including that of our Lord.

From our own time:

1.   Take a selection of simple coloured pictures of people at work. Make a collage of perhaps A4 size; stick this firmly to card which can be cut by the children. Other backings can be used, of course. Cut the picture into interesting shapes—the smaller the child, the larger the pieces!

Marked and kept in small plastic bags, these home-made jigsaws can be passed round and used many times.

'Thank you, God, for work and for people who work for us.'

2.   (a)   Growing-up: do the same with pictures of baby, child, teenager, adult; keeping in sequence will help in the understanding of the process.

 (b)   Ask them to bring snaps of themselves; get the children to slot these into a piece of card, one for each child, allowing plenty of surround. Fix the corners at the back with Sellotape. Draw frames or patterns round the snaps and add a name. Then, leaving the photos whole, cut out in various shapes. Put into a plastic bag, it's ready for someone else to 'put me together'. (Old holiday snaps are good for this.)

From the time of Jesus:

1.   Take a picture from one of the published sets of Jesus' life or teaching; placing it on another card, turn it into a jigsaw—make sure the two are stuck firmly together, perhaps as part of your preparation! With a limit to its viewing-life, a build-it-up-yourself picture takes on a new dimension. Kept in bags, it doesn't need to be hung and can be used many more times.

2.   Draw your own picture, and do the same.

Fun to make, these home-made jigsaws can illustrate teaching on any subject: Jesus, Bible, Church, people, life. They are also a good class stand-by and a good calmer-down on arrival!

Don't forget the teaching point of jigsaws, however. For life is rather like them. As we grow up we are always adding new pieces to the picture of ourselves. When we are old we can think of our lives as being made up of the many pieces we have put together ourselves, sometimes with the help of others and always with the help of God.

Dear Father God, We thank you for helping us to put together all the parts of our lives. We will try to make them interesting, cheerful and worthwhile. We are grateful, too, for the help of other people.

As Jesus always saw the jigsaw of peoples' lives, we ask our prayer through him. Amen.